MACHINE LEARNING FOR BUSINESS

TABLE OF CONTENTS

DISCLAIMER

ABOUT THE AUTHOR

George Pain is an entrepreneur, author and business consultant. He specializes in setting up online businesses from scratch, investment income strategies and global mobility solutions. He has built several businesses from the ground up, and is excited to share his knowledge with readers.

WHAT ARE MACHINE LEARNING AND ARTIFICIAL INTELLIGENCE?

How an Algorithm Works

To understand what machine learning is we first must know what an algorithm is and how it works. Most programming is actually based off of mathematics and it is thanks to a man called Turing that we have computers in the first place. Turing built a state reserved system or rather a system that preserved and used the current state of the system in order to do calculations. Most of this is unknown to the public beyond the fact that it was this machine that helped to break the famous German Enigma codes during World War II. Algorithms come from mathematics and this is the reason why we are able to translate algorithms into programming languages because programming languages are based on mathematics. Therefore, the more mathematics you know, the stronger your programming skills are likely going to be.

An algorithm, or a function, represents a step by step process on how to take inputs or variables and turn them into output or result variables. The term variable represents the fact that the data inside of the variable is changing or can be changed. Result variables are results that are changing or can be changed, which is why a having a state preserved machine is so important when it comes to programming. In programming, a function will take in variables and make decisions on it before it either returns more variables based on those decisions or provides your final output. This is how, conceptually, algorithms work inside of programs. This is the core of how machine learning works.

How a Recursive Algorithm Works

Whenever we talk about recursive algorithms, we are talking about algorithms that call on themselves until they get to the desired result. The primary example utilized for this is the Fibonacci code. You have to continuously call on the function in order to produce a series of numbers that will ultimately give you the Fibonacci code. However, since the Fibonacci code can be somewhat complex and confusing for most individuals, I have found that I often have a better chance of showing what a recursive algorithm is by simply working through a string. Since a string is literally a set of ASCII characters that have been displayed using a reference format, you can iterate through them much like you could elements inside of what is known as an array, which is like a grocery list. Below, you will find a recursive algorithm that iterates through a single string but calls on itself each time it needs to go to the next character.

```
example = "Hello" # array of characters
recursive_marker = 0 # current location of characters
def recursive_function(string, count)
    i = string.length # setting a stop location/number
    if(count <= i) # only runs if there are more characters in a string
        puts("    " + string[count].to_s) # prints each letter to the string
        count += 1 # increases current location of characters
        recursive_function(string, count) # recursive call
    end
end
recursive_function(example, recursive_marker)
```

```
H
e
l
l
o
```

Neural Networks

A neural network, the hard-coded machine behind the concept of machine learning, is a series of if statements that can be as big as you want them to be but ultimately handle the feature of the problem that

4

you want to solve. Most of the time, these neural networks are designed to handle complex features that require severe amounts of processing power in order to complete them, such as recognizing faces or the products that they are searching for inside of an image. With a neural network, you have inputs (such as a massive amount of data that you would normally not be able to search through on your own), you have your neural network (which represents the different markers that you are looking for inside of that data), and finally you have what is known as your output as a result of this data.

Recursive Neural Networks

Just as you saw with the recursive algorithm that I displayed for you, neural networks can also be applied in a recursive manner. The reason you would want to do that is something called the fading gradient. This refers to the fact that data can get so complex and neural networks can have so many connections, that the neural network itself is what slows down the overall process and makes it worse than a regular algorithm. Normally, this creates a problem for any type of machine learning that requires anything more than three layers of neural nodes. The reason recursive neural networks were created was because of the concept of convoluted neural networks, which we will talk about later on.

Essentially, each neural node is connected to the neural nodes that came before it. Therefore, whenever you have a neural node on the network and you have three layers of neural nodes on that network with one node per layer (so you would have 3 and 1 layer and then 3 in the second layer). You need to take into consideration that it is a factor of x every time you go to the next node in the node network. Therefore, if you start out at the first node, you are only connected to one node. However, when that node goes to the next node in the neural network, that next node will have 3 nodes connected to it. When it goes to the next node in the network, it will have 9 nodes connected to it. When it goes to the next node in the network, it will have 81 nodes connected to it. The next node will have 6,561 nodes and then that next will have 43,046,721 and then that next will have 1,853,020,188,851,841. As you can see, this number gets extremely huge extremely fast and massive neural networks simply aren't possible without recursive algorithms to slim down the number of neural network nodes that are connected together.

What is Machine Learning?

Machine learning is literally the process of everything I just described above with the addition of utilizing a decision tree which we will talk about later. Essentially, the data goes in one section and gets filtered through the different neural nodes on the neural network to produce a result on the other end of the network. If that result is not what is expected, we then look at the neural network to see if any problems occurred. If no problems occurred inside of the network then we know that the data set might either be bad, or we may not have considered all of the variables. On the other hand, if the neural network is incorrect then we add what are known as biases and weights so that we can get closer to the answer (this may need to happen several times to get the expected result). This is the learning part of machine learning whereas the machine part is the fact that a machine is doing it.

What is AI?

AI, otherwise known as Artificial Intelligence, is not the same thing as machine learning, and I find it very frustrating that people seem to confuse the two. Although machine learning is a form of AI, it is not the only form of AI. Artificial intelligence is the ability to fake intelligence. Video games have been doing this for decades because first-person shooters need enemies that can provide them with a challenge. In video games, this artificial intelligence is represented by what is known as a field of view variable where if a person's X & Y coordinates are within a certain radius from the enemies' X & Y radius, then the enemy automatically moves towards the person's coordinates. Additionally, if they are within x amount of range then the enemy character starts attacking and doing damage regardless of whether they would logically be able to do damage in real life if they were facing that position. This creates a sense that the enemy can kill the player because they are intelligent, but it has only simulated the intelligence that we have ourselves.

Machine learning, on the other hand, performs tasks that make it seem like the machine is intelligent, but the machine is only capable of doing that task because we took time to tweak algorithms to get it to that exact result. It's kind of like saying that a spear is intelligent because it never fails to pierce flesh but if we were to try to use a spear for anything else, it would be difficult if not completely impossible. The same is said of an image recognition machine that seems intelligent until you try to apply it to crunch the stock market numbers. It is faked intelligence that seems to be intelligent to us.

WHAT IS A PREDICTIVE MODEL? WHAT DO THE SCORES REPRESENT?

What is a Predictive Model?

A predictive model is a model that takes in information and makes a prediction based on the data that has been given to it. In fact, there is an entire industry based on predictive models called statistics. We would not have statistics if we weren't interested in predictive models because statistics do the same thing but on a much more manual level. A predictive model looks at the data and generates a mathematical formula that will help you to predict what is likely going to happen at different future time intervals based on the information that it is handed. You can do this with statistics, but you would have to do it by hand whereas predictive modeling is usually done by the computer.

What is the human equivalent of the Predictive Model?

The human equivalent of the predictive model is most noticeable in your local weatherman because your local weatherman uses a predictive model all the time. They feed the collected data into a predictive model to try and predict what it's going to be like over the next X amount of days. Organizations also do this whenever they are attempting to see when crime is rising or falling, detect when situations may be getting out of hand, and when business revenues seem to be going up by most of the numbers but through predictive modeling you can figure out that sometimes the numbers can be deceiving as we will see in the next chapter. It is important to know that predictive models are forms of neural networks that have been pre-designed to predict equations based off of linear data and so you may need a different solution if you have nonlinear data.

What do the scores represent?

The two most known predictive models are nonparametric and parametric models. Parametric models assume that you know where one of the parameters is causing most of the change in your data, and so nonparametric data represents one that you don't know where it is. Nearly all neural networks that are out there on the market can be utilized in a way that provides you with a predictive model, but those are the two most common types of models inside of the predictive model genre. The scoring inside of a predictive model is really representative of what you're trying to do with the predictive model. For example, a credit card company could set up a scoring system with a predictive model that judges the successfulness of an individual to be able to pay for the credit that they loan them based off of their past transaction history.

Where are Predictive Models Used?

Predictive models are used whenever you are talking about applications, simply because it works wherever anything can be predicted. Some examples are crime rates, financial decisions, work performance, and the list really goes on for where this type of neural network can be used. In fact, it is used on a daily basis to not only tell you what the weather is, but it will also be used to run the traffic lights in major cities to ensure that there are less rush hour traffic accidents, and to determine the likelihood that an area will be affected by current traffic models. The list really does go on when it comes to predictive models and where they are used.

USING A PREDICTIVE MODEL TO MAKE DECISIONS

Gathering Data

Let's say that you have decided to use some predictive modeling software, but you don't see the true benefits of it. After all, no machine can truly be that good at predicting the future to where this is such a vital tool, right? The first step is that we collect our data and let's say that our data looks something like this.

```
-----------------------------------------------------------
| Initial Sale | Percentage | Customer Count | Revenue |
-----------------------------------------------------------
           00           00               00         22
           03           08               08         49
           04           12               05         48
           11           05               05         48
           08           09               07         53
           07           11               06
           11           12               04
           10           09               06
           08           08               07
           10           04               08
           05           05               07
-----------------------------------------------------------
[Finished in 0.2s]
```

Taking a Guess at It

Now, it's obvious I'm doing my standard programming here, but I want you to take a stab at guessing what the next few numbers will be. What, difficult? Yeah, it should be because you just see a bunch of numbers. But you should also see that we receive a base revenue of 22 for some reason, so that should help. What, you can't think of one? Well, to be honest, I didn't expect you to because all you see is a ton of numbers and it is difficult to tell what the correlation between them might be. If we were to just guess on what's going to happen just based off of revenue, we could say we might see an increase, but we are more or less going to see the chart go down one for the next to and rise by a few points for every third one. However, as you will see, this could prove erroneous.

Noticing the massive change

There are a number of software solutions out there for you but in order to create this environment, I needed to make sure that I had full control over both ends so I programmed this in by hand. What would normally happen is you would have a spreadsheet of numbers, such as a csv, and this would then be fed into the software that would produce a prediction as well as the exact algorithm it used to achieve that prediction. I already have that algorithm on hand.

$$23 + i + p + (c * 2) - 1$$

As we can see, this equation is simplistic by nature, but let's see what the full sheet looks like:

```
-------------------------------------------------------------
| Initial Sale | Percentage | Customer Count | Revenue |
-------------------------------------------------------------
         00            00            00            22
         03            08            08            49
         04            12            05            48
         11            05            05            48
         08            09            07            53
         07            11            06            52
         11            12            04            53
         10            09            06            53
         08            08            07            52
         10            04            08            52
         05            05            07            46
-------------------------------------------------------------
[Finished in 0.2s]
```

What we now see is that not only does the revenue stagnate, but in the last week, this ultimately results in a significant drop in revenue. I say that this is significant because it drops below the point where we first began to feed data into the system. Imagine if you had made an even worse prediction in a real-world environment! If you hadn't used a predictive model, you would be telling your bosses or yourself that you would expect revenue to have a slow rise when you would actually see a massive drop. Image if this were in the millions. $6 isn't much but $6,000,000 is a ton of lost revenue and this was a good scenario, something that wouldn't ultimately cause people to lose jobs.

WHAT ARE DECISION TREES?

How a Program Works

Decisions trees are very similar to programming, and how a singular program works can be sufficiently complicated enough. For a program, you must first write the code in order for the program to start up with all the necessary variables. Then, the code is based on how the user will interact with the program, and sometimes there are multiple levels of IF statements that help control the flow of functionality for the user so that the user just isn't looking at a giant list of functions that they can use without some guidance on how to use them. You might think of Photoshop as a good example because Photoshop has a section called filters where you have a selection of different types of filters that do different types of things but all of them are sorted into subcategories that you can choose sub-items from. Now, the only problem is that a program only makes a decision based off of the user input and so as much as you may be nesting all of the complexity of the logic, you are still waiting on the user to make the final decision in this puzzle.

How You Make Decisions as a Person

The honest truth is that you use decision trees all the time, but you don't realize it because you utilize it as a natural process. Decision trees are really good at breaking things down whenever you have multiple choices and you need to decide the best choice in that case. Normally, you can make a decision tree graph that will help you make a relatively uncomplicated choice such as what type of application development you want to undertake or what type of television show you want to watch. You make these decisions without the conscious use of a decision tree because most of the time our brain has already gone through the decision tree at that point. This is because we are accustomed to needing to make decisions within a few seconds to a few minutes until our brains naturally break things down into if statements, which is why we have them inside of our programming, so that the brain can then deduce whether it wants to go with one decision, another decision, and so on and so forth. Whenever you make a decision tree, you are simply elaborating on the flow that it took you to get to such a decision, but you leave out the decision because it is up to the computer to get to that decision based off of what's inside of the decision tree.

How a Decision Tree is Made

There are three components to the most basic of decision trees. You have decision nodes that take you to the next label or feature, the root node/label that starts everything, and, finally, the leaf nodes that represent your results based on your decision nodes.

The Ultimate Goal of a Decision Tree

The ultimate goal of a decision tree is a two-part goal depending on what you are hoping to achieve with the tree. The first part is that if you are planning to have your tree come out with some ultimate result that matches a correct answer, then the ultimate goal is to get a decision tree that is capable of taking large quantities of inputs and giving the correct output most of the time. On the other hand, if you are doing the second part, and that is feeding data in to hopefully create a decision tree that can give you some sort of result that you don't know yet, then the ultimate goal is to whittle the unnecessary information down to the point where you can extract useful information at usable quantities. This is the ultimate goal of the decision tree and it really matches how we work as human beings.

Let us take a survival situation as an example. Whenever you make a decision as a person in a survival situation you are either making the decision based on an outcome you previously saw, an emergency manual that you hope will hold true, or you are just using the information that is the most useful to you at the time to make an ultimate decision, otherwise known as an educated guess. As you can see, a neural network is very similar to how an actual brain works and so you can utilize it to conquer many of the things that the brain naturally does but at the speed of a machine.

NEURAL NETWORKS AND DEEP LEARNING

Some Types of Neural Networks

Feedforward

Feed-forward networks are really simple to understand because they simply mean networks that you put information into so that it can go in a linear direction represented as forward inside of the network. This was the first type of neural network ever developed before we began using something known as backpropagation.

Autoencoder

An autoencoder is rather weird whenever you describe it to the average individual because the purpose of this type of neural network is to feed it input so that it can break that input apart and see if it can put the input back together. This is the most famous type of neural network when it comes to unsupervised learning because you don't really need to keep an eye on it and feed it data that is specifically geared towards beginning steps. You just feed it data and see if it gets the correct data out again and change it if it doesn't.

Probabilistic

This type of network is usually utilized for pattern recognition and it actually has four different layers; it has an input layer, pattern layer, summation layer, and an output layer. The pattern layer relies on the radial basis function to determine the distance of your current test case from the neural node by utilizing the sigma values. The summation layer serves as a hidden layer that will help summarize which category the pattern best fits into per case. The reason why this type of network exists is that it's usually faster than the beginning neural networks that we used to have such as multi-layer perceptron networks, and is a lot more accurate when it comes to predictions and excluding any outliers.

Time Delay

If you have live data coming forward and you need to feed it immediately into a neural network, the time delay neural network is built for this type of data. The way a time delay neural network works is that it usually a has a perceptron network that has been developed by using back propagated connection weights and it forcibly delays the amount of time that it takes a specific neural node to give an output.

Convolutional

A convolutional neural network is currently the most popular type of neural network that's out there for machine learning. What it does is utilize the concept of convolution, which is where you utilize two separate functions to figure out what you need for a third function to work or to be generated from those two functions. There's a lot of applications that utilize the convolutional concept of a neural network. You know it for image and video recognition, but it's also used in Google Voice as well as any systems that might be recommending something to you.

RNN

The most common type of neural network that's out there is the recurrent-neural-network. There are several different forms that this neural network can take but the principle aspects of this type of neuron that work are really easy to understand. This is a feed forward type of network that can go backward at certain steps to reprocess information. The most common example of where we use this is our spelling correction programs that look at previous words in the sentence to determine if that word is incorrectly spelled or grammatically incorrect.

Modular

A modular neural network is a neural network that's made up of several other different neural networks. The reason why you might want to have this is if you need text recognition on top of image recognition in the same neural network to analyze a single picture. There are several reasons why you might want to combine these networks and there are several different types of modular networks. However, they all follow the same definition as being a network of other smaller neural networks.

The True Meaning Behind Deep Learning

There seems to be this mystique behind deep learning that a lot of people fantasize about, but deep learning is a really simple concept and is nowhere near as mystical as is made out to be. Deep learning simply means that the neural network that you are working with has more than one layer of neural nodes to it to further increase the amount of machine learning that is occurring. In fact, the full name for deep learning is deep machine learning. The reason why it represents more than one layer of neural nodes is that the information goes *deeper* into the neural network in order to produce the results that you are looking for. We developers really need to think about the names that we label things because the same thing happened whenever computers came around and people were somewhat afraid of touching them. Now we have Terminator references popping up again.

HOW TO USE DECISION TREES

Using Digit Representation

It's important to realize right off the bat that a computer does not recognize the words yes and no. Instead, we computer scientists have come up with the clever trick of using 1 for yes and 0 for no. The reason this is important is that all your features and your output results are going to be represented as numbers and not anything that would normally be recognizable to the human eyes such as a literal answer to your question. Similar to the reason why the answer to life is 42, we must first recognize that the computer is not going to be able to speak in sentences unless you're building that type of network, and then, of course, it will be able to speak in sentences, but that doesn't mean it'll speak in sentences that you can understand at first. Instead, you need to have a numerical representation of every output that you plan to have. So, if you were to have 6 different types of output then you would choose maybe the numbers 2 through 8 since 0 and 1 represent true and false, or yes and no.

Choose Your Desired Outputs if Possible

Some of us are without the benefit of a desired output so sometimes the output is just a random jumble of numbers that we need to make sense of. But most of us require that a machine learning algorithm actually do something that we want it to do. For instance, a good machine learning algorithm is the facial recognition machine learning algorithm. The end goal was to detect faces inside of images, so all our output would be a square around where the image was but in the form of numbers. Therefore, the lower numbers represented areas that didn't likely have a face inside of it whereas the higher numbers represented an area where there was likely a face in it. As I already said before, machine learning algorithms are designed to work with numbers and not literal items unless we are talking about big machine learning algorithms that took months to develop such as the convolutional deep neural network. This is the type of network that Facebook currently uses in order to detect the faces inside of our pictures.

The Main Decision Gets the Ball Rolling: Root Node

The first thing that I'm going to do is I'm going to generate a bunch of random numbers so that we have a data set to work with. I am not entirely sure what our data set is going to give us but I'm going to make the decision to filter out most of the results and this is what is known as the root node. Here is the algorithm to generate this dataset of random numbers between 1-100:

```ruby
container = []
1000.times { container.push(rand(100)) }
print(container)
```
```
1, 98, 20, 45, 93, 78, 66, 19, 30][Finished in 0.2s]
```

Now, I will not show the numbers of the dataset because it would take up a ton of space when I don't need to take that space. However, I believe our root node is going to filter out whether the number is below fifty or above fifty. I'm going to refrain using complex Ruby code here simply because I know that most Data Science is done in Python and R, I just like Ruby. This is what the code is for making the root node as well as the result:

```
1   container = [48, 36, 64, 46, 31, 69, 96, 25, 61,
2   # adding 1 to index 2 means it was below 50
3   # and adding 1 to index 3 means it was above 50
4   results = [0,0,0,0]
5   for i in container
6      if(container[i] < 50)
7         results[2] += 1
8      else
9         results[3] += 1
10     end
11  end
12  print(results)
```
`[0, 0, 472, 528][Finished in 0.2s]`

Why did I leave the first two open? No real reason. What you will learn in Data Science is that you want to have as much data as possible going in and coming out so having a larger result array is usually preferable.

Nodes in Your "Network": Making Decisions

Bias

Adding a bias to the system is similar to adding a weight to the system but it represents a different aspect of the system. Whenever you are introducing a bias to the system that means that you know that the results are likely going to be wrong. In the method that we have up here, we don't need to add a bias. But if we were to do something like image detection or something much more complicated where we don't actually know that we are just dealing with random numbers, then we would likely use a bias so that as we recursively developed our machine learning algorithm, we could change the biases to effectively bring the result closer or further from the expected result by changing the bias and utilizing the bias in the final calculation. The goal is to have a very simple equation that allows you to get a number and then based on the importance of that node, we want a certain bias from that node to affect the result. This is why almost all biases start off with a null or 0 value so that they don't affect anything before you begin to change things. When you get an outcome that you didn't expect, you go through the biases and see which one of the nodes would have likely caused that inappropriate outcome to happen and change the bias to see if you can get that node to give you the correct outcome. Most of the time, you will not be changing the core logic of each of the nodes but rather the bias and the weights of the nodes.

Weights

The weight of a node really just represents the importance of that node in the neural network. If you have important data that you want to utilize immediately then you put it in the important node area, which is why different nodes have different weights. Additionally, biases and weights allow you to keep track of where data is traveling in the neural network so that when something unexpected happens you can look back at the results of the weights and the biases to see where it could have possibly gone wrong.

Feature

A feature represents the logic behind a specific node or collection of nodes. When we implemented the logic of testing to see if our number was below or above 50, we created a feature that described the value of the number. Features represent important questions you want to ask about the data to get the ultimate outcome that you are expecting or that you hope will occur. I'm going to go ahead and add some additional logic and the goal for my code is to test whether the numbers in our array are truly random.

```ruby
container = [48, 36, 64, 46, 31, 69, 96, 25, 61, 1
=begin
adding 1 to index 2 means it was below 50
adding 1 to index 3 means it was above 50
adding 1 to index 4 means it was below 25
adding 1 to index 5 means it was above 25
adding 1 to index 6 means it was below 75
adding 1 to index 7 means it was above 75
=end
results = [0,0,0,0,0,0,0,0]
for i in container
  if(container[i] < 50) # Main Feature
    results[2] += 1 # Leaf Node
    if(container[i] < 25) # Decision Node
      results[4] += 1 # Leaf Node
    else # Decision Node
      results[5] += 1 # Leaf Node
    end
  else
    results[3] += 1 # Leaf Node
      if(container[i] < 75) # Decision Node
        results[6] += 1 # Leaf Node
      else # Decision Node
        results[7] += 1 # Leaf Node
      end
  end
end
print(results)
```

[0, 0, 472, 528, 226, 246, 268, 260][Finished in 0.1s]

33

Getting Results: Leaf Nodes

Now that we have most of the logic done for this *extremely* basic non-biased non-weighted neural network, we need to make our final decision. A final decision is made in a similar manner, but it has two overall components. The Confidence variable represents just how sure the program is of the prediction that it is making, while the Prediction is the actual True or False Decision of the program. Therefore, we are going to add one more open element to our results array and use the first two elements in the array to provide a Random or Not Random result. We'll go ahead and move this into its own separate method.

```
31  def confidence_and_prediction(results)
32    bias = 50
33    confidence = 0
34    if((results[2]/2 - bias) <= (results[3]/2) and (results[2]/2 + bias) <= (results[3]/2))
35      if((results[4]/2 - bias) <= (results[5]/2) and (results[4]/2 + bias) <= (results[5]/2))
36        if((results[6]/2 - bias) <= (results[3]/2) and (results[2]/2 + bias) <= (results[7]/2))
37          results[0] = 1
38          # mostly sure
39          results[8] = confidence + 75
40        else
41          results[1] = 1
42          # not sure
43          results[8] = confidence + 50
44        end
45      else
46        results[1] = 1
47        # mostly sure
48        results[8] = confidence + 75
49      end
50    else
51      results[1] = 1
52      # sure
53      results[8] = confidence + 100
54    end
55  end
56  confidence_and_prediction(results)
57  print(results)
```

[0, 1, 472, 528, 226, 246, 268, 260, 100][Finished in 0.2s]

Now, as you can see, we got a Random Variable back with

100% confidence. However, since I know that I used a Random

function, I know that my machine learning algorithm is wrong. There

could be several areas where I did something wrong. For instance, my

decision nodes have several things wrong with them, or holes if you

will.

1. Do I really need to divide everything in half? This is a useless

    step.

35

2. Will there always be a definite case where the number is definitely going to be both below or above the second result if I add my bias? It would be more likely if I put an "or" there.

There may be some additional bad logic in there, but I'm going to fix what I see and show you the array.

```
[1, 0, 472, 528, 226, 246, 268, 260, 75][Finished in 0.2s]
```

Suddenly, by changing the code to fix some of the bugs not only did I get a correct answer, but I am also aware that if I use "or", then either one or both cases could be true, and this could be problematic. However, since I got a positive result here, I would generate another random array to test that array and if it was wrong then I would change the logic, bias, and confidence even further. So, as you can see, this is not only how you make a decision tree but also how you start a neural network. This one just so happens to be testing whether or not something is random.

Making it Look Nice

Up until this point, we have been looking at an array, but this is what the data scientist will see and if you have more categories then you likely do not want to be stuck looking at some numbers on the screen. Therefore, you may choose to print something out like this:

```
-----------------------------------------------------------
Random: 1
Not Random: 0
below 50 : 472
above 50: 528
below 25: 226
above 25: 246
below 75: 268
above 75: 260
confidence score: 75
--------------------------------------------------[Finished in 0.1s]
```

So, why should we do this? Well, for one, it allows us to visualize the data much better and to understand our final results. Additionally, if we see something odd then we'll be able to see it immediately like this. Finally, we do this for people who are not us and do not understand arrays.

HOW TO USE BIG DATA FOR BUSINESS

Precise Marketing

Let us say that we are a coffee shop that sells coffee in New York City. Do we really want to advertise our coffee across the nation, or do we just want to advertise our coffee to the people of New York City in a fashion that only the people of New York City would be able to understand? Machine learning is capable of acquiring the living areas where individuals who purchase your product currently reside, and where the majority of individuals that buy your products are located. Never before have we been able to collect this type of data so quickly and so readily because people often have no problem giving out their address to companies who develop applications for instantly paying at the location they are buying from. The reason why this is important is that marketing has begun to evolve over the past two decades. National television, television that usually was either carried over cable television or radio towers that sent out free channels, charges a massive fee for advertisements to be displayed on the television nationally.

When something like YouTube came out, we started to gain access to advertisements in a localized area such as the United States of America, rather than Canada or Mexico, which could have been utilizing the television network as it expanded into other countries and didn't only include cable television and free channels via radio signals. Once we started getting access to regional advertising, Facebook began to localize the advertisement to specific individuals who fit categories that we wanted to advertise to. Google, once again, took this even further by localizing the advertisements to the neighborhoods that we wanted to advertise to.

Machine learning has the potential to take the next step in this evolution by analyzing the customers in your database along with the provided addresses to figure out exactly which houses buy the most amount of product from you, and which houses buy some product but could buy more product. As you can already see, having such knowledge would give you access to the people you primarily want to advertise to, that you are likely to see the most success with the least amount of cost. Businesses spend millions of dollars on advertising, and

as we have seen through the sponsorships on YouTube, marketing has become cheaper and cheaper as people with giant audiences don't mind agreeing to smaller amounts of money to advertise a product to a category of people.

Product Creation

As our machines get more complicated and our technical parts become so complicated that it is difficult for an organization to create most of those parts, machine learning takes a step forward by being able to crunch the numbers that we, as humans, are not capable of crunching. A good example of this is the quantum computer that was developed a while back and is now solving some of the biggest problems in our history because regular computing simply can't perform the tasks of these calculations at the speed at which Quantum Computing can. The problem is that we don't all have access to Quantum Computing. That doesn't mean that if we had access to Quantum Computing it would be useful to us.

Machine learning is all about mimicking the human mind and finding a way for the usefulness of the human mind to run at the speed of the computer mind. When we develop new products through upgrades, we must make design and engineering choices based on what can provide the best upgrades. These choices are mathematically broken down into specific sciences that one can study and develop to create enhancements that are very alluring. Remember that if a machine can study a certain area by using mathematics, such as the ones that I just mentioned, it can do the job better and faster given enough examples and development time. This suggests that future smartphones and other products that require a specialist viewpoint might be created by machine learning rather than an individual simply because the requirement to develop these machines is so high that only machines are capable of conceptualizing them without any help from others.

Feature Selection

When we talk about features as normal human beings, we are talking about items that make up an entity, and we are technically talking about the same thing whenever it comes to machine learning.

However, when we talk about features inside of software development we are often talking about special tools that the user can use in order to get some type of task done.

A good example of this is Photoshop because Photoshop has a ton of features. One of the features of Photoshop is that you can crop images so that you can remove any unwanted background from an image whether it is with a box crop or if it is selecting the background through exact precision. This would normally be considered a feature of the program and the honest truth is that a lot of time is spent in developing these features because these features ultimately determine the user experience that an individual has inside of an application. Hundreds of hours are spent on upgrading software so that it has the newest features that you can possibly have to create the best user experience that it can possibly provide. Needless to say, if you hand over the information about the largest number of complaints that a user base has about a piece of software, and the largest number of requests from a company to develop certain features, you can shorten the amount of work needed to figure out which features should be in the new upgrade so that more time can be spent on making those features. However, in a very scary sense of the word, we can also **develop** these features using machine learning. If a machine learns how to code a feature, then it is possible for a machine to learn how to get the end result we are looking for out of that feature and then provide us with the necessary code to insert into our program. This is scary because it essentially replaces the need for any type of web developer, software developer, and pretty much anyone that isn't a data scientist. That is a lot of people. We are talking about nearly half the higher education job force.

Locate Issues Before They Become Massive

I suppose the last benefit that comes out of machine learning is that you can locate your issues before they become a massive problem. This is the case if you have developed a machine learning algorithm correctly. There is a quality assurance process known as Six-Sigma that allows companies to track down problematic situations causing the productive workflow of an environment to slow down. If a machine learning algorithm were to be taught the Six-Sigma techniques, and were to successfully implement a Six-Sigma environment so that it can begin measuring the different variables, we can now say that we would have program that could effectively track down a problem causing instance before it became big enough for us to notice. The reason why this is beneficial is that it helps to prevent things like salmonella poisoning, worker injuries, and a ton of other problems that come with the physical manufacturing and inspection of products. Additionally, the products that we would produce would actually increase and so a company would be able to sell more and thus gain more profit as a result of having a machine learning algorithm that was capable of maximizing the productivity range of the environment that they've been deployed to.

NEW TECHNOLOGIES IN MACHINE LEARNING

Machine Learning in Games

Developers over in the Asian countries have begun to place machine learning inside of their games because machine learning offers the capability to enrich the game experience by simulating actual conversation. While the size of the deep-learning network is small (because you would have to deal with the volume of players that are online at any given time so the calculations would be out of this world) these conversations are primarily centered around providing a natural feeling to the conversation a player is having with an NPC, and additionally finds new ways to entice their consumers into purchasing additional content that they like based off of their interactions with the neural network. This has a significant impact with things like customer service and sheds light on an almost entirely new industry with machine learning because now consumers can provide producers with a much better understanding about what they want out of the producer company.

Sophia: AI Workers in a new Light

Sofia is a robot that is so sophisticatedly built that Saudi Arabia granted Sofia citizenship. The dilemma behind Sophia is one of the few different key points that is currently affecting Saudi Arabia. Of course, the very first thing that a lot of people don't like about this action is that Saudi Arabia already has problems with giving rights to women. A woman has to be with a man if they are to give a public speech, and several other rules apply simply out of sexism because they believe that a woman is incapable of being on her own. The reason Sofia is a problem here is because Sophia seems to have more rights, and because she looks like a woman, they automatically judge her based off of her appearance rather than based off of what she is, which is a robot. However, it also brings into perspective the possibility that AI may no longer be machines that simply do one task, but are capable of doing multiple tasks and have citizenship. This brings up the question as to whether an AI should be paid for the work that it does, and it blurs the line between Robotics and Humanity.

Social Media Responses

A few companies in the past year have learned why you should always test something before you decide to use it, as they have begun to develop machine learning so that more accurate audience targeting social media messages can be sent out over social media networks, essentially replacing the need for a social media manager. The job of a social media manager is to study the business and the social feeds along with their interactions to see how they should interact with the audience of that social media account. These new machine learning algorithms suggest that it is possible to remove this job and represents a new product that companies can sell to each other when it comes to marketing by having more advanced machine learning algorithms provide better responses to consumers interacting with the business through social media applications.

Development of Materials Fabrication and Processes

Part of the problem with creating new materials in this day in age is the amount of research that needs to go into creating them in the first place. You see, when a new material needs to be created, the normal way to do this is to scour the academic journals to learn how other similar materials were made, and determine if there were any missing combinations of components that can be used to develop the new materials, and the process to develop them. It takes, potentially, hundreds of hours just to find a new material and then an equal or slightly less amount of time to develop a new process to make that material. MIT is putting together a machine learning algorithm that will search through all the digitized forms of research to not only suggest materials to be made, but also the process in which to make them.

FeatureHub by MIT

Another addition to the machine learning community is the addition of a tool utilized by MIT. This tool will allow machine learning enthusiasts to develop features for other machine learning scientists. Let us say that you are having difficulty coming up with features for a current problem that you were dealing with but the old methods of creating features with the help of others required that you go to each one individually and hope that they didn't also want to do the project. Now, the tool that MIT provides will allow individuals to go onto a website and submit their problems so that other machine learning scientists can suggest features for them to utilize or options on how to solve the problem. This is a first for machine learning scientists.

Azure and Amazon AI

One problem that has cropped up for many of those who would like to participate in the active machine learning community is the amount of processing power that is required to perform large-scale data processing. These require huge machines that cost a lot of money, but most scientists are not rich, especially if those scientists are either just coming out of school or are hobbyists. As a solution to this answer, Microsoft and Amazon have both created their own products to provide the capability of machine learning. Microsoft has created an Azure machine that can allow you to quickly formulate a decision tree for your neural network to go through and visualize that decision tree in the same action. Amazon, on the other hand, is a little bit more open-minded by providing a platform that gives you the hardware. but not the actual tools that you are working on. The primary choice is to utilize Tensor Flow, but you also have access to Frameworks of your choosing such as torch, theano, and Cafe 2.

ETHICAL USE OF MACHINE LEARNING FOR BUSINESS

Minority Consideration

Whenever we develop any type of machine learning or any type of algorithm for that matter in America, we also tend to only account for the white individuals of the population simply because they make up most of the population. Now, I'm not here to say whether this is going to be true going into the future, but the problem is that we develop our systems based off of this imaginary bias. The problem with only utilizing white individuals as the basis for our calculations is that it doesn't take in the minority as a consideration, and this is true of developing anything with the bias of either a Christian or a Muslim because these two religions make up the majority of the religions in the world. By not taking into consideration the minority individuals in the world, we begin to make machines that have holes in them. A good example is the debacle that Google had a little while ago with its learning machine because women had an extraordinarily high amount of search queries for black individuals. Because Google didn't account for the persistent problem that the black community has with jail time and being persecuted by the police, Google began suggesting background searches and police searches whenever the search was related towards male individuals who were also black. This led to several hurtful, hilarious, but also troublesome titles that would say that the Google search algorithm was racist because they suggested the background and jail time searches for black men. Technically, you could also say that that was sexist, but you can't really say that the political discourse at that time was too concerned with sexism.

Now, why is such an aspect important when it comes to developing machine learning for businesses? Well, the truth is that when businesses develop machine learning it's usually to handle a process that's very massive in its size and scope. An example might be trying to recruit individuals online. If you are looking for a personality that matches more towards white individuals than black individuals, or you are searching through an industry that is usually full of white individuals more than black individuals, then the data that you feed it will begin recording the traits of the two different groups. But since you gave it more of one race than the other, it is a possibility that the machine could learn to only associate the good qualities with the white individuals of the data set that you provided. This is just a small example of how not including minorities as an equal part of the test can eventually disrupt the correct answers you're looking for inside of the machine learning.

Guessing Accuracy

It may be convenient to utilize machine learning in a situation where the answer needs to be the best answer based off of data and the data is so big that your average scientists can't digest it all before you need to make a decision. A good example is if a mudslide is occurring or if a tornado is in the area and you need answers very quickly. In terms of business, a better answer to this type of example would be if you need to make a decision on whether it is a good idea to open up to the public or to stay a private company, or even whether you want to sell a certain product in a very controversial market. It is increasingly important to make sure that the guesses that you get out of machine learning are accurate guesses because when you rely on machine learning to give you numbers to cover the market, you want a general sense of correctness in those numbers. If your machine learning is ever used to do anything important, you want to make sure that you have taken the steps to give your neural network as many correct answers as it can possibly digest so that you know that your machine learning algorithm is giving you the correct choices. While some of the examples I used would mean that you would profit from getting the best correct answers, you also have to realize that in a case where machine learning is used to tackle a very large and vast problem, you would want to make sure that you were making the correct choice based off of the correct data, such as in the case of firing an employee because the employee might be the reason why your company is not being as productive as it could be, or they could very well not be. Let's say that you have a thousand employees on staff and you noticed that the productivity levels have significantly decreased over the past week. You have an idea of who it could be, but you want to use machine learning to look at all the variables and see what machine learning gives you before you decide to fire the employee because the employee fulfills a role that is difficult to replace. Therefore, you begin trying to design this learning machine to figure out how you could pinpoint the source of a problem and who is responsible for the tasks that are not being taken care of. However, because you have an idea of who it is, you begin changing the algorithm to pinpoint the reason why you think it might that be that individual. Suddenly, your machine learning algorithm is saying that it is correct because it has detected all the external biases you have put into the machine. In this case, your belief that a specific somebody was the result of the problems in your company caused you to create a learning machine algorithm that would only target that type of person, rather than target the actual person who might be causing the problem. This means that you used the learning machine to fire an individual that doesn't need to be fired and so next week, when you notice that you have the same problem, you won't know what went wrong because you'll think that your machine was designed correctly and that you made the correct decision, even though you fired an individual based off of a machine that was designed to pinpoint that individual and not provide an accurate guess.

Developer Bias

This actually brings me to my next topic because whoever develops the machine learning is going to have certain biases whenever it comes to choosing the data. For instance, they may not be particularly racist, but they could only choose black individuals as their dataset or they could choose only white individuals as their data set without even realizing that they're doing this. It is vitally important that you always make sure that the individuals that are making your learning machine are of separate backgrounds because we all have our individual vices and underlying biases that affect how we implement systems. If we don't take into account the fact that we are all different, then we end up with systems that exclude the individuals who are different. It is important for not only those who are going to be affected by this machine learning algorithm to have a part in it and to have a say in it; but also to reflect on to you and what it is going to do for you.

Delegating Proper Priorities

It is vitally important for the entire system that develops this machine learning algorithm to realize that the entire picture is important and that the variables that you were looking at are not the deciding factor of the system. A lot of people who set out to develop a machine learning algorithm ultimately are setting out to develop a system to detect one item but what you need to realize is that if you set out to detect one item then you're going to miss the big picture and sometimes, as a result of narrowing your viewpoint, you actually miss some of the factors that would help you target what you want to target. This is why it's very important to clearly define what your system is going to do by looking at the big picture rather than a very narrow and selective set of information. When you go through something like supervised machine learning, you are teaching it to gradually get better and better at getting the end result that you want. But if the result that you want only takes into account one specific thing, then it is likely that some information that is important to that one specific thing will get lost across the journey that the data has to take. By setting a very clear goal and by ensuring that your machine learning algorithm takes in the larger picture, it can accommodate for the greatest number of issues so as to make a machine that is more robust and capable of handling more than that one thing should you decide to expand its uses.

Digital to Physical Implementation Impact

Let us say that you developed a machine learning algorithm that removes the need to write down material. There is absolutely no need for anyone to write any more after you create this machine learning algorithm. Better yet, let's just go ahead and expand on this and ensure that no one would need to schedule anything anymore because you have created an application that is capable of listening to your wants and scheduling them perfectly. Not only that, but it can take all of your files and organize them for you and call people to set up meetings. Now that we've created this awesome machine learning algorithm, what happens to all of the secretaries in the world? A secretary is supposed to write things down, be able to follow the individual who they work for, schedule meetings and call people to set up those meetings, and finally, organize the files. This machine that you have developed will essentially replace the need for having a secretary and since having a secretary is usually a luxury, we can't really say that a secretary is absolutely vital or a special skill in most cases. Therefore, not only is the position not absolutely vital to run a company but you can also avoid paying an individual for the spot of being a secretary because you can have a machine do it. In fact, this is something that happened whenever several scheduling applications came out that could also pull up personal files. The truth of the matter is that while we may not have replaced all secretaries, there was a significant impact because we created a technology that did somebody else's job. Additionally, a secretarial position doesn't have anything it can translate into unless you want to add some extra skills on to it, and so all of the secretaries that were fired because an application was capable of doing their job had to go into different fields of work in order to compensate for their lack of a job. Some of these secretaries had been doing their job for nearly two decades.

Now we are even thinking about automating truck driving using driverless trucks, all the truckers on the road that normally earned anywhere from $15 to $20 an hour will be out of a job with only trucking as their experience. This is another job that represents a position that doesn't translate very well into other positions and that if we replace them, thousands of individuals will be out of work.

This is something that a lot of people are pointing out and the fact of the matter is that when you decide to utilize digital tools to impact physical performance, you need to make sure that the impact that you are going to have is a good one more than it is a negative one. Replacing the thousands of individuals who would normally have a job with a robot simply because it costs a company less is not exactly an ethical decision. This means that whenever we provide a digital solution, we also need to think over the physical impact that solution might have if we were to introduce it to the world on a mass scale so that we can handle the ramifications.

Turing Ethics

The case of Sophia brings up a very interesting point inside of computer science and machine learning because Sophia is the first robot to receive citizenship in the world. I often tell people that the reason why Sophia received citizenship, beyond the advertisement of Saudi Arabia as a technology hub in the world, was also to prevent possible problems that one could come across, ethically, with developing these AI systems. If you have ever watched any futuristic movie that had a dark theme to it but also included robots that were capable of human interaction, then the usual side joke would be that men would have access to robotic women that would provide services that normal women would not provide. The truth of the matter is that if we treated these systems as tools and gadgets rather than the potential sentient beings that they might become, we might honestly turn this fantasy into reality. I'm not saying that this is a particularly bad thing but, at the same time, if you are a married individual and your particular religion says that you cannot commit adultery, but you have intercourse with a robot, does this count as adultery? Is robotic prostitution any different than actual prostitution? We often see robots as tools that are designed to help us, but we also have carnal desires and a lot of individuals see advanced robotics as a solution to the rejection of others. Now that

Sofia is a citizen, she is protected by law from acts of adultery and similar cruel experiments that would be performed on machines that are not performed on humans. Her citizenship prevents the people working on her from doing anything to her that would not normally be done to a citizen of Saudi Arabia. Like I said, her situation is very interesting because it brings up a lot of questionable ethics when we imagine the future of advanced robotics. If a robot is capable of being confused with a human, should we give robots the rights of humans such as a minimum wage? Should we develop an industry of robots that are specifically set to an AI level that is not capable of sentience so that we can still have non-citizenship robots? How far can a machine learning algorithm go before we can effectively say that if we go any further then the machine will gain the right to have citizenship? This is a very huge question when it comes to business because the more advanced we make our robots; the more jobs and skills can be performed by those robots. Therefore, all businesses looking into machine-learning need to keep this in mind if they plan on making machines capable of replacing workers.

Evil Intentions

Just because you build the most beneficial machine learning algorithm that exists doesn't mean that somebody won't try to make sure that you cannot share it with the world. As a business, we need to make sure that we develop security around the machine learning algorithms that are put in control of vital systems. Machine learning algorithms can handle what the human condition can't compensate for, but if we make machines capable of handling these vital systems then we also need to make sure that these machines can't be targeted. After all, we have seen over the years that no matter how beefy the security, there will always be a hole in it. Since we are making these machines of code, we need to make sure that the code that we write has as few holes as possible and has as many layers of protection as we can possibly build around them. Likewise, we need to pay very close attention to how much the machine learning algorithms have control, and whether there is an oversight of that control or not.

AI Control

This actually leads to our next topic as to whether we should allow AI to control certain aspects of our lives. It is a real possibility that the robots that we develop could gain the knowledge needed to recognize us as parasitic rather than beneficial to the survival of living creatures. There will come a time where humans are no longer able to comprehend the amount of complexity that's inside of a robot and whether we control that complex robot or not is essential in knowing whether the human race will still be alive x amount of years from now or not. An AI system could easily self-develop to replicate itself so that it could take out its creators because its creators can ensure that the robot is no longer living. So, if we create a machine learning algorithm that understands self-preservation, then we might have some trouble ahead of us. Needless to say, it's very important to gain a control on just how complex an AI can get.

CONCLUSION

While this may be the end of the book, it is nowhere near the end of what neural networks are and how you can begin to deploy them yourself. There is a ton of information out there on neural networks and how to utilize them along with cutting-edge algorithms that are suggesting newer forms of machine learning. As a courtesy to you, I have included all of the code that I used at the end of the book so that you can have access to it. I hope you enjoyed reading this, until next time.

```
=begin
adding 1 to index 0 means that it was Random
adding 1 to index 1 means that it was not Random
adding 1 to index 2 means it was below 50
adding 1 to index 3 means it was above 50
adding 1 to index 4 means it was below 25
adding 1 to index 5 means it was above 25
adding 1 to index 6 means it was below 75
adding 1 to index 7 means it was above 75
index 8 is the confidence score
=end
results = [0,0,0,0,0,0,0,0,0]
for i in container
        if(container[i] < 50) # Main Feature
            results[2] += 1 # Leaf Node
                if(container[i] < 25) # Decision Node
                    results[4] += 1 # Leaf Node
                else # Decision Node
                    results[5] += 1 # Leaf Node
```

```
                end
        else
                results[3] += 1 # Leaf Node
                        if(container[i] < 75) # Decision Node
                                results[6] += 1 # Leaf Node
                        else # Decision Node
                                results[7] += 1 # Leaf Node
                        end
        end
end
def confidence_and_prediction(results)
        bias = 50
        confidence = 0
        if((results[2] - bias) <= (results[3]) or
(results[2] + bias) <= (results[3]))
                if((results[4] - bias) <= (results[5]) or
(results[4] + bias) <= (results[5]))
                        if((results[6] - bias) <= (results[3])
or (results[2] + bias) <= (results[7]))
                                results[0] = 1
                                # mostly sure
                                results[8] = confidence + 75
                        else
                                results[1] = 1
                                # not sure
                                results[8] = confidence + 50
                        end
                else
                        results[1] = 1
                        # mostly sure
                        results[8] = confidence + 75
                end
        else
                results[1] = 1
                # sure
                results[8] = confidence + 100
        end
```

66

```ruby
end
def print_result(array)
    puts("-"*64)
    puts("Random: " + array[0].to_s)
    puts("Not Random: " + array[1].to_s)
    puts("below 50 : " + array[2].to_s)
    puts("above 50: " + array[3].to_s)
    puts("below 25: " + array[4].to_s)
    puts("above 25: " + array[5].to_s)
    puts("below 75: " + array[6].to_s)
    puts("above 75: " + array[7].to_s)
    puts("confidence score: " + array[8].to_s)
    print("-"*64)
    end
confidence_and_prediction(results)
print_result(results)

example = "Hello" # array of characters
recursive_marker = 0 # current location of characters
def recursive_function(string, count)
    i = string.length # setting a stop location/number
    if(count <= i) # only runs if there are more
characters in a string
        puts("    " + string[count].to_s) # prints
each letter to the string
        count += 1 # increases current location of
characters
        recursive_function(string, count) # recursive
call
    end
end
recursive_function(example, recursive_marker)

# code for predictive model

data =
[[0,0,0],[3,8,8],[4,12,5],[11,5,5],[8,9,7],[7,11,6],[11,1
```

```ruby
2,4],[10,9,6],[8,8,7],[10,4,8],[5,5,7]]
def
predictive_solution(initial,percentage,customer_count)
    return (23 + initial + percentage + (customer_count
* 2) - 1)
end
puts("-"*55)
puts("| Initial Sale | Percentage | Customer Count |
Revenue |")
puts("-"*55)
data.each do |x|
    for y in x
        print(" "*8)
        print((y < 10 ? "0"+ y.to_s : y.to_s))
        print(" "*4)
    end
    print(" "*8)
    print(predictive_solution(x[0],x[1],x[2]))
    print(" "*4)
    puts("\n")
end
puts("-"*55)
```

www.ingramcontent.com/pod-product-compliance
Lightning Source LLC
Chambersburg PA
CBHW070855070326
40690CB00009B/1848